AF261293

Prompts That Make Kids BEG to Write!

by Judy Bruns

Coco Publications

Published in 2016, by Coco Publications

Coldwater, OH 45828

Copyright @ Judy Bruns

All rights reserved.

No part of this book may be reproduced or utilized in any form or by means electronic or mechanical including photocopying, recording, or any information storage and retrieval system, without written permission from the publisher.

Bruns, Judy

Prompts That Make Kids BEG to Write!

Written by Judy Bruns / Design by Andrea Bruns

ISBN

978-1- 4951-7442- 1

Library of Congress Control Number: 2016949730

Edited by Erica Ranly

Book Design by Andrea Bruns

Book Setup by Jessica Vassar

PRINTED IN THE UNITED STATES OF AMERICA

Table of Contents

Dedication

*For all young authors-to-be, who need only the sparks of encouragement,
inspiration—and sometimes a bit of fun—to kindle a love for writing.*

Special Thanks

*Thank you, Erica Ranly, for your clever suggestions during the layout of this book.
Once my student, you've become your teacher's favorite mentor!*

Introduction

Prompts That Make Kids BEG to Write!

The topics in this book are wide open for students' interpretation, details, and expansion. While most of the topics tend to engage kids through a connection with humor, other topics allow students room to pour out their hearts about the people, experiences, beliefs, and events that have already impacted their young lives.

I hope the teachers who use this book will motivate their students to come up with creative, fresh approaches to the prompts. Students need to be challenged to capture their reader's attention with vivid mind pictures, on-target descriptions, and action words and to write realistic dialog that makes the personalities of the characters come alive! Of course, teachers who write along with their students—and share their stories as students share theirs—have an optimal effect on bringing enjoyment to the writing classroom.

My goal is to get students so excited about writing that they will look forward to the topics of the day and to picking up that pen or pencil to let their stories flow. I hope, too, that teachers who use this book will find within these pages some *Prompts That Make Kids BEG to Write!*

Big Blunders!

- Our family bought a house in Alaska online. . . but it turned out to be an igloo!

- Sorry! I didn't know you were wearing a wig!

- The dentist pulled the wrong [patient's] teeth!

- *Tomorrow* is pajama day at school, not today!

- Ah oh! Great-grandpa's ashes got sucked up in the sweeper!

- I watered Mom's flowers with her energy drink by mistake. Guess what happened!

- That wasn't dog shampoo! Grandma was getting ready to color her hair!

- Next time, please advise all farm children that Show & Tell does not include [pet pigs]!

- Stop! You're tearing down the wrong house!

- Who forgot to close the cage door?!

Changed!

- The game is no longer the same; the rules have changed.

- What an amazing MAKEOVER!

- The twins switched places again!

- When my 13-year-old brother opened his mouth to sing, his voice had changed!

- Phooey! Get that diaper changed!

- Space command has changed our rocket's course! What's going on?

- When I asked for change for a $100 bill, I was handed 10,000 pennies!

- I had aged overnight!

- Someone changed the road sign!

- This can't be my dog! She's not the same.

Could Be Inspiring

- He/She gave me someone to look up to.

- I learned from that experience that it's not always about me, after all.

- The fastest runner in the school was now competing in a wheelchair.

- She had never seen snow before.

- I sat there for an hour just watching the ants in their own little world.

- The reward would be mine someday, just not right now.

- There in front of me was the snarling, but beautiful beast!

- My eyes are more precious to me now than ever before.

- The wrinkled hands were clasped together in prayer.

- What's important becomes clear when you're homesick.

What Do You Mean by That?

- I'll never fit into her shoes.

- Don't leave Earth without it.

- Feathers fell from the sky.

- Finally, he was safely home.

- We're missing our tackle!

- I was framed!

- Now it was up to the judge.

- Oh, no, here comes another drill!

- "Teacher, may I wear eye shadow on our *makeup day*?"

- It was all about "big bucks."

Did Someone Say "IDIOMS?"

- I couldn't afford it—it cost an arm and a leg.

- My goose is cooked!

- Sometimes it's just a dog eat dog world.

- Eating humble pie isn't easy when you've bragged that you're the best.

- I was beginning to connect the dots.

- They were throwing money out the window.

- Sometimes daily routine can become a rat race!

- That salesman was crooked as a hook!

- Leah broke into tears when we told her to break a leg.

- He/She led a dog's life.

Do I Smell a Mystery?

- The secret lay hidden beneath the creaky floor boards.

- Would the tracks lead to the suspect?

- The flashlight's beam shone directly on a face.

- Who, or what, stood on the other side of the door?

- It appeared to be falling from the 32nd floor.

- A suspicious birthday card arrived in the mail.

- The contents of the secret room left us breathless.

- Grandma's bifocal glasses were on the nightstand, but where was she?

- It was a case of mistaken identity.

- Gee, you look just like this picture on the "Missing Persons" poster.

Follow the Orders!

- No, you may not go toilet papering!

- Shh! Be quiet or the thief will hear us.

- Spit it out!

- I ordered my steak "well done," not so rare it could run!

- Lock the doors!

- Don't eat the paste!

- Get in line!

- You can't use Dad's shaving cream till you have whiskers!

- Just stomp on it!

- Throw it in the garbage—fast!

Go Figure!

- Yesterday we had plain old gray squirrels in our backyard, but today they're [orange].

- I won the losing ticket.

- In our family we have no "hand-me-downs," only "hand-me-ups."

- Everyone was sleep deprived after the sleepover.

- It was broken, but saved, for a reason.

- There's a pack of wolves in front of you, a lake behind you . . . Escape!!

- When I gave the clerk a 10 dollar bill for a gallon of milk, he gave me $97.50 back in change.

- It started with a quarrel and ended with a handshake.

- The boy/girl played "Mozart's Symphony No. 40" perfectly on the piano—with no hands!

- When I looked out my window this morning, the familiar scene was gone!

Have Fun with This One!

- Where's the pacifier? This baby's throwing a fit!

- I put my tooth under the pillow, and guess what I got!

- I was duped!

- It wasn't an ordinary trampoline.

- It stuck on the ceiling, and it won't come off.

- Spare me from the smelly socks!

- This insidious pimple won't get off my nose!

- Stay back! It's ONION BREATH!

- It made me itch all over.

- Bubblegum and braces do not get along!

Headline News Stories

- "Baby Speaks Early—A Month Before Birth!"

- "Local Genius Disappears After Inventing Time Machine"

- "Missing Camel Seen Heading for Sandbox!"

- "Skunk Causes Panic at Rodeo!"

- "Skateboarder Gets Stuck in Fresh Cement"

- "Terrible Odor Shuts Down Whole Town"

- "Local Inventor Makes National News"

- "Unlikely Hero Comes to the Rescue"

- "Helicopter Drops Dollar Bills All Over the City"

- "Movie Patron Finds Surprise in Popcorn!"

Memories

- It was my favorite hiding place when I was young.

- A special person used to sit in that chair.

- That song brings back memories.

- They remembered making mud pies when they were young.

- I was "crushed."

- It was the BEST Christmas gift. . . one I would never forget giving!

- Grandpa/Grandma told me about the "good ol' days" when he/she was growing up.

- The happiest memory of my childhood, so far, is when. . .

- Dirty handprints used to cover the bathroom towel.

- I can still remember when I was learning how to _______ .

One-Word Topics!

• Contagious	• Nosey
• Grounded!	• Scat!
• Lockdown!	• Irreplaceable
• Saved!	• Boom!
• March!	• Testing

Questions for Starters

- Are you saying your paper was accidentally deleted?

- How did this 10-foot-wide hole get in our garage roof?

- How do you say "no" to a big, brown bulldog with begging eyes?

- How was I going to explain the smashed rotten eggs?

- In the ring stood the matador, but where was the bull?

- So, how did you get such a weird nickname?

- What more could anyone ask for?

- Where did all this dirt, dust, and crud come from?!

- *Who's* piloting the plane?

- *What* did the dog drag home this time?

Serious and Thoughtful

- Bruises heal, but some take longer than others.

- It became my phobia.

- It started with greed.

- That experience would stay in my mind forever.

- Forgiving/Being forgiven isn't always easy.

- Perhaps some things that are caged shouldn't be.

- Shortcuts can be expensive.

- Sometimes the truth hurts.

- While they had no great beauty, brawn, or brains, they had something just as importan

- Hands touched the keys for the very last time.

Here's Something to LAUGH About!

- Grandma's teeth are removable!

- Aunt Edna looked unusually "stylish" in her orange, spiked hair!

- Be careful what you say to a parrot!

- I requested a "booster seat," not a "booster shot!"

- I went in for a haircut and came out bald.

- Some practical joker put a sock in my trumpet!

- They used cottage cheese to frost the cake!

- Out popped his glass eyeball, into my bowl of soup!

- It's B-R-I-A-N, not B-R-A-I-N !

- This canine catches flies!

That's Different!

- He/She rode the lawnmower to school every day.

- They're looking for a white dog in a snowstorm.

- Lunch at the "hotel" featured spoiled milk and stale crackers.

- Splendida Katrianna Blankenship can't fit her name on the line!

- My new friend is Will Power.

- My little brother eats bugs!

- We came to a red, yellow, and *purple* traffic light.

- Dad reluctantly agreed to take dancing lessons—till the grass skirts arrived in the mail!

- Zoo alert! A moose is on the loose, and a chimpanzee is riding on his back!

Winner of *WHAT?*

- Elvis Look-Alike Contest
- Milk Guzzling Match
- Freckles Contest
- Coupon Queen Award
- Knuckle-Cracking Marathon

- Ostrich-Riding Race
- Cutest Toothless Smile Award
- National Burping Event
- Lemon-Eating Contest
- Winner of (Writer's Choice!)

Double Trouble!

You have 20 rather than 10 choices!

- I'll NEVER use freckle-removing cream again!
- It was a Jell-O fight—and out of control!
- Don't hit the skunk!
- The plumber installed our new bathtub in the wrong room!
- This is what happens when they've had too much candy!
- One too many zeros can get you in trouble.
- Who put glue in my hair?
- Grape juice doesn't look good on white carpet.
- Hopscotch uses chalk, not permanent marker!
- There must be a grade card mix-up!
- It just broke . . . all by itself . . . really.
- It was my first job, and I mowed the wrong lawn!
- Never again would they call, "Here, kitty kitty," in the jungle!
- That was the WRONG can of spray!
- The dog got into Grandpa's vitamins.
- X-rays show that the surgeon left something behind!
- Two steaks came up missing from the grill.
- Water balloons ready? Fire!
- Stage fright!
- Toddler + lipstick = trouble

Surprise!

- You bought a secondhand jacket and found something in the pocket!

- Whoa! Somebody buttered the playground slide!

- "Welcome to class! We're having a Pop Quiz today!"

- There's a moving package on our doorstep!

- Where did this $$$ come from? My billfold is filled with cash!

- When I opened my eyes, everyone was gone!

- There's a peculiar sound coming from the garbage can.

- No swimming today! Hundreds of frogs are surrounding our pool!

- There's a pearl in my oyster stew!

- There's a tunnel beneath our house!

- This is definitely not your "typical" museum!

Tips for Teaching "Story Writing" Effectively

DON'T SCARE OFF THE KIDS!

Use the words "narrative" and "story" interchangeably! The kids will feel more at ease—and more capable—when you tell them that "narrative" is simply another word for "story."

GIVE YOUR DAILY WRITING SESSIONS A "CATCHY NAME."

Here are some examples:

- "Fastwrites"
- "Quickwrites"
- "PowerWrites"
- "Story Sparkers"
- "Story Launchers"
- "Jumpstarts"

Regardless of the catchy name you choose, I suggest that you give the students 4 topics a day to select from.

HOW LONG DO YOU SPEND TEACHING NARRATIVE WRITING?

Think "4-4-4."

- 4 topics to select from daily (with 2 minutes brainstorming/12 minutes to write)
- 4 sessions a week
- 4 weeks for story writing sessions

BE ENTHUSIASTIC AND CREATIVE!

If the teacher is bored, the students will be bored for sure! Build suspense!

- Cover up the 4 daily topics on the board as the students enter the classroom.

- Don't uncover them until you have introduced the day's topics (see examples below) and the students are dying to see them!

- Read the prompts with excitement!

How to introduce the daily topics. . .

- "Hold onto your seat! Are you READY for this?!"

- "Is your imagination 'pumped up' today?"

- "Get that creative brain in gear!"

- "You're going to absolutely LOVE (picture of a heart or a smiley face) today's topics!"

- "Today's topics should be banned from school because they'll be TOO MUCH FUN!"

- "You'll be begging for more time to write today!!"

DISCUSS DIFFERENT WAYS TO "APPROACH" THE TOPICS!

After uncovering the prompts, spend a minute or two discussing the topics you've put on the board for the day. Give students examples of different ways to look at the topics. For instance, consider the prompt,"*Drill*." As the teacher, you might ask—

"Are we talking about someone getting a tooth drilled at a dentist's office?"

"Could the story be about a fire or tornado drill at school?"

"Do you want to write about someone drilling after discovering oil on their property?"

"You might want to write about a construction worker's drill that seems to have a mind of its own and digs holes where they're not supposed to be!"

"You could make your story's problem involve a military drill, a spelling drill, or a crime suspect being drilled with questions!"

WISE COUNSEL!

Tell your writers that. . .

- stories need to have a problem;

- stories need to have a climax, a point of greatest anticipation or suspense;

- the problem (usually!) gets solved BELIEVABLY by the end of the story.

Advise your students to use the 5 "W's" and the 1 "H" as guides as they develop interesting characters and add descriptive details to their story.

The 5 "W's" and the 1 "H"

Who?

What?

When?

Where?

Why?

How?

PRE-WRITING
BRAINSTORM! BRAINSTORM! BRAINSTORM!

Brainstorming is absolutely essential! Invite the class to jot down their ideas in web form, in linear form, "scribble picture" form, or whichever way is best for them.

- Set a timer for 2 minutes, and tell the kids that, when you say "Go!" they will have only 2 minutes to brainstorm their topic!

- When the timer goes off and they beg for another minute or 2 to brainstorm, reset your timer, and—[ahem!]—reluctantly grant your students' request!

- I've concluded through my years of teaching that the creative brain works well under pressure! However, if you have a student who struggles and works at a slower pace, by all means, make adjustments for his or her success.

MODEL THE BRAINSTORMING STEPS FOR YOUR STUDENTS

- On the board, on paper, or by using techie equipment, show your students how it is done.

- Pick a topic, one of your own or a topic from this book, and brainstorm it, saying your ideas out loud as you jot them on the board into a brainstorming web or other brainstorming format.

- Another modeling technique, at least when you first start your Fastwrite sessions, is to declare one of the day's topics for whole-class brainstorming. In other words, brainstorm the topic together as a class and build the framework for a story.

NOW---LET'S WRITE!   (Beat the power of the blank page!)

As with brainstorming, time your students, again, as they actually start "power writing" their stories. Give them 12 minutes to write, but when the timer goes off, *allow* [wink! wink!] a few extra minutes when they beg for more time to write.

CATCH YOUR READERS' ATTENTION FROM THE VERY BEGINNING OF YOUR STORY AND "LOCK 'EM IN."

Here are some common methods:

- Start in the middle of the story and then backtrack/flashback to the beginning.

- Start with an unusual statement that gets explained in the course of your narrative.

- Start with dialog. (Don't we all just love to tune in to others' conversations?)

- Begin with a question that eventually gets answered or addressed in subsequent paragraphs.

- Refer to a famous quote, or to a common saying that you hear around your house, that connects with your story.

- Start off with the main idea or the lesson that you will be trying to get across in your story.

- Begin by describing a central character, the background and the time, or the location where the story takes place.

CLEVER, SURPRISING-BUT- SEEMINGLY-BELIEVABLE TWISTS IN A NARRATIVE ARE ENGAGING.

However, avoid having too many subplots in a short story. There is neither time nor space for development. Short stories are termed "short" for a reason; they're brief and tightly-worded with one main problem to be solved.

Be attentive to your goal. Focus on developing and solving the problem so that your story will lead your reader to a logical conclusion.

REMEMBER TO INCLUDE ONLY A FEW CHARACTERS BY NAME.

Again, there's little time and space for development in a short story. You'll want to put your best effort into making those few characters "real" to your reader through direct and indirect characterization.

Show what your characters are like. . .

- by what they say.
- by what they do.
- by what others say about them.
- by others' reactions toward them.
- by directly describing them.

USE "ON-TARGET" WORDS!

This is particularly important with short stories. Since they use far fewer words than a novel-length story, your words need to be carefully chosen BUT NOT NECESSARILY THE FIRST TIME AROUND IN YOUR ROUGH DRAFT.

- Your ROUGH DRAFT writing piece should be quickly written the first time around, capturing the ideas "roughly" as they pop into your head. Remind yourself that there will be time for perfection later.
- It is when you revise and refine your story that you insert the perfect on-target words and descriptions that more closely say what you mean.

WRITE AN EFFECTIVE, BELIEVABLE ENDING!

- Leave no "loose ends."
- Leave no contradictions between what you say in your story and the way you end it!
- Leave your reader with a feeling of completion.
- Remember that CLEVER endings can have impact, BUT. . .
- Be sure your story's ending sounds believable!

After 4 days of "Fastwrite" class sessions, tell your students to do the following:

- Select your favorite rough-draft narrative from the ones you have written over the past 4 days.
- Complete it if you didn't before.
- Have it proofread by your student group.
- Revise, polish, and type it, with the final copy due by (designated day) for a grade.

Consider giving students Day 5—Friday—to work on their final Fastwrite in class. Don't be surprised if you hear students say they are not only completing their favorite narrative for the teacher, but that they are also polishing some of their other unfinished Fastwrites, besides, because they just can't leave their stories alone!

SHARING---AND BEYOND!

- Once graded narratives are returned to their creative writers, students read their stories within their proofreading group. Group members are expected to comment on the improvements other students have made on their writing pieces!

- Finally, each group nominates one of their writers to stand up and read his or her narrative to the whole class. After each group's elected reader finishes, anyone else in class who wants to read is invited to do so, providing time allows.

SHARING---AND BEYOND (continued)

When students come up with exceptional writing pieces, encourage them to try to get their stories published in a children's, teen's, or education magazine. Two great resource books I've used for finding publishing addresses are *Children's Writer's & Illustrator's Market* and *The Christian Writer's Market Guide*. Be sure to use the most recent copies of each book that you can, because publishing companies that are listed could change owners, addresses, and names—or close their doors—over time. Places that publish children's writing pieces can be located by doing an Internet search, also. An example is *Amazing Kids Magazine*, an online magazine for kids 8-12 years old. Go to http://mag.amazing-kids.org/get-involved/write-for-us/ to check out the website.

GRADING YOUR STUDENTS' STORIES:

Some teachers will want to score the typed narratives holistically; others might prefer a rubric. (A sample rubric can be found on the next page, p. 32.) Your evaluation method will, hopefully, place special emphasis (more weight or points) on the skill you focused on during your 4-day, weekly session.

Sample Rubric for Scoring Fastwrites

Ideally, writing should be scored on the basis of the writing standards and learning goals that were set up by the teacher at the beginning of the writing lesson. For example, if creativity has become the primary goal, then creativity needs to be the main focus for scoring the writing piece. If the aim is to write an effective introduction, then points given for an effective introduction need to reflect that. If the teacher is looking for conclusions that make stories sound complete, then scores should be based on how well students achieve that goal. Another consideration in scoring a writing piece might be the mechanics (grammar, punctuation, capitalization, spelling, etc.). Do the mechanics help make the story understandable, or are the errors distracting? Total points will vary, depending on a number of factors. Some teachers might decide to use a check system rather than points for each measure below.

Final Fastwrite Rubric   Score: ___

Creativity and Development

__Satisfactory/Appropriate/Amusing title

__Introduction engages reader's attention

__Basic info. handled well (5 Ws/1 H: Who? What? When? Where? Why? How?)

__Story development (makes sense as the story unfolds; no gaps; fine transition)

__Writer's voice (Sound believable? Understandable? Interesting? Consistency in style?)

__"In-character" dialog

__On-target word selections

__Conclusion makes story sound complete

__Sufficient length to tell the story

Mechanics

__Grammar

__Punctuation; Capitalization

__Paragraphing

__Spelling

__Avoidance of unnecessary repetition

Appearance

__Double-spaced

__12 pt. font/Times New Roman (or similar)

__1" margins (except top of first page)

Afterword

What would it be like to live in a world devoid of creative spirit, engaging stories, shared feelings, and humor? Boring! Hopefully, the prompts in this book have motivated kids to get excited not only about writing, but also about sharing their writing pieces with others!

About the Author

Judy Bruns has been published in hometown and Christian newspapers, in magazines and other publications. She is a retired language arts teacher and Power of the Pen writing coach.

Her children's picture books include *Donnie Lost in the Cornfield*, *Hattie and Her 43 Cats*, *Now I'm a BIG Girl*, *Now I'm a BIG Boy,* and *Painting Grandma's Nails*.

www.ingramcontent.com/pod-product-compliance
Lightning Source LLC
Chambersburg PA
CBHW042123030726

47599CB00002B/325